This edition published by Parragon Books Ltd in 2016 and distributed by

Parragon Inc.
440 Park Avenue South, 13th Floor
New York, NY 10016
www.parragon.com

Written by Claire Sipi
Illustrated by Emily Golden

ISBN 978-1-4748-1474-4

Printed in China

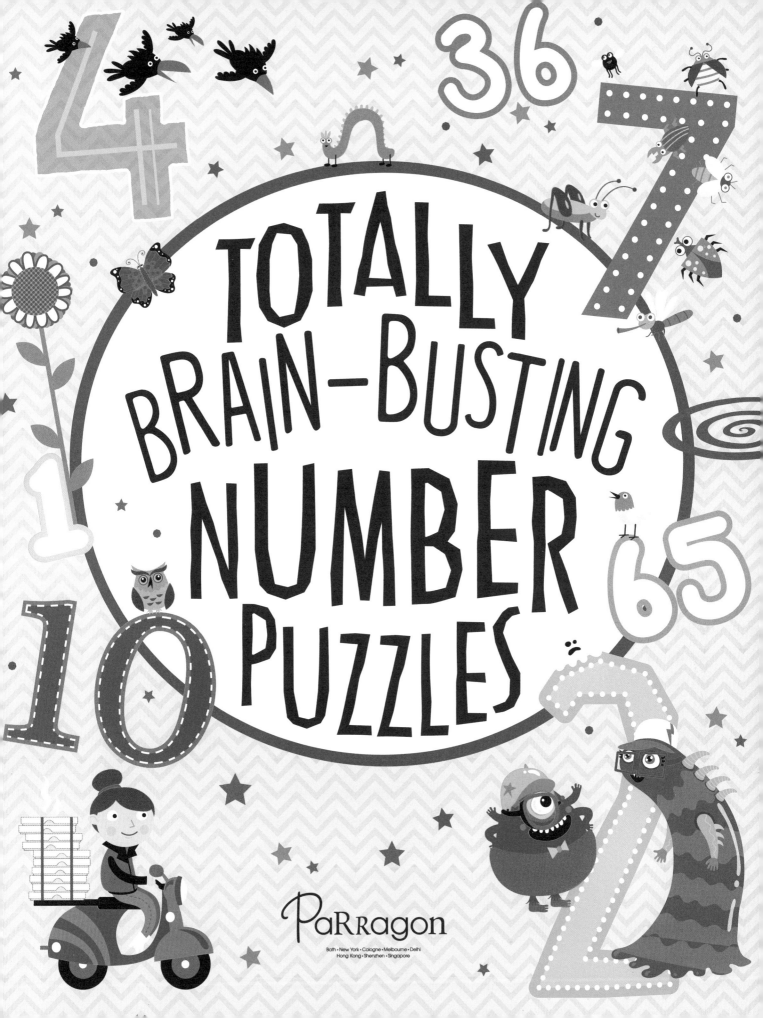

TOTALLY BRAIN-BUSTING NUMBER PUZZLES

PaRragon

Bath • New York • Cologne • Melbourne • Delhi
Hong Kong • Shenzhen • Singapore

Follow these directions to find the treasure!

START

How many gold coins
do you think we'll find in
the treasure chest, matey?

2   8   3   6

10   11   ◯

◯   ◯

Fill in each blank
by adding up the two
numbers above it.

◯

Fill the chest with treasure!

5 x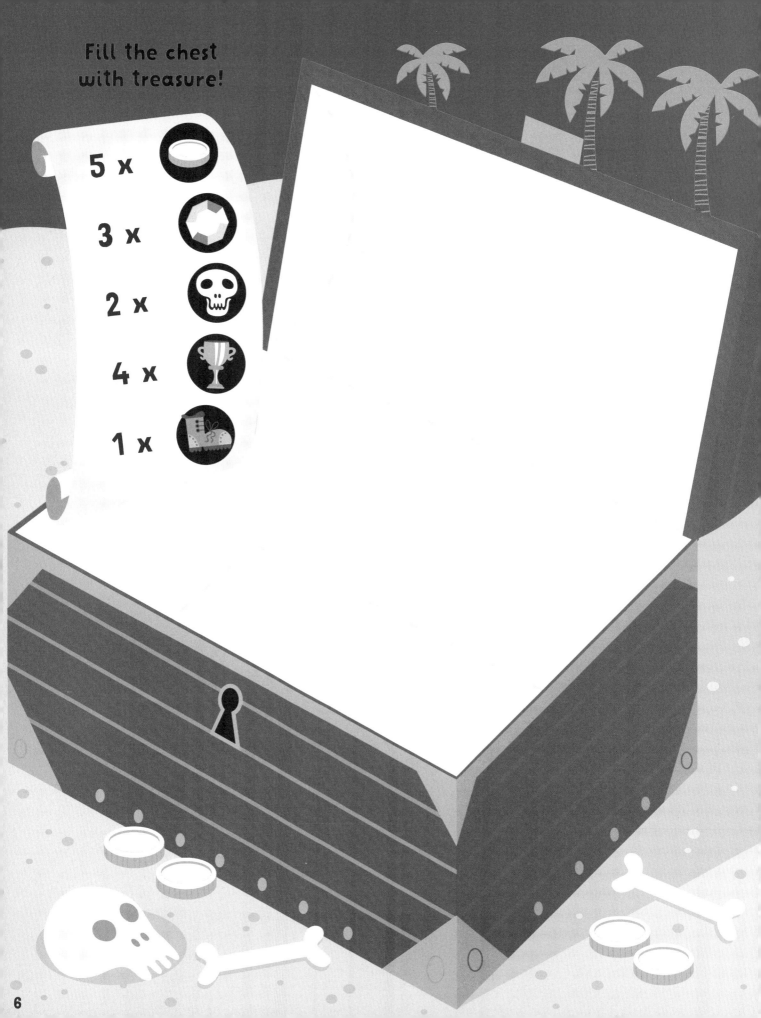
3 x
2 x
4 x
1 x

I need **6** clubs to juggle, but I only have **2**!

START

8

The show is about to start,
and the juggler is late!

FINISH

Oof! I can only carry things that add up to a total weight of **10**!

Draw in the missing items!

Fill in each blank club by adding up the numbers in the balls on either side.

Let's help these butterflies get to the flowers in the right order!

92 76

46 92

39 21

21 46

Matching wings need to be next to each other.

Use the color key below to finish the flowers.

1 3
2
4 6
5

13

Time to spread some joy!
Now ... who do I need to find?

2 grumpy gnomes

3 frustrated fairies

4 unhappy elves

Magical! Look
who's at the end
of the rainbow.

Do you remember the way back to the campsite?

Yup! We follow the trees with an odd number of pinecones. We can go up, down, left, or right at those trees.

START

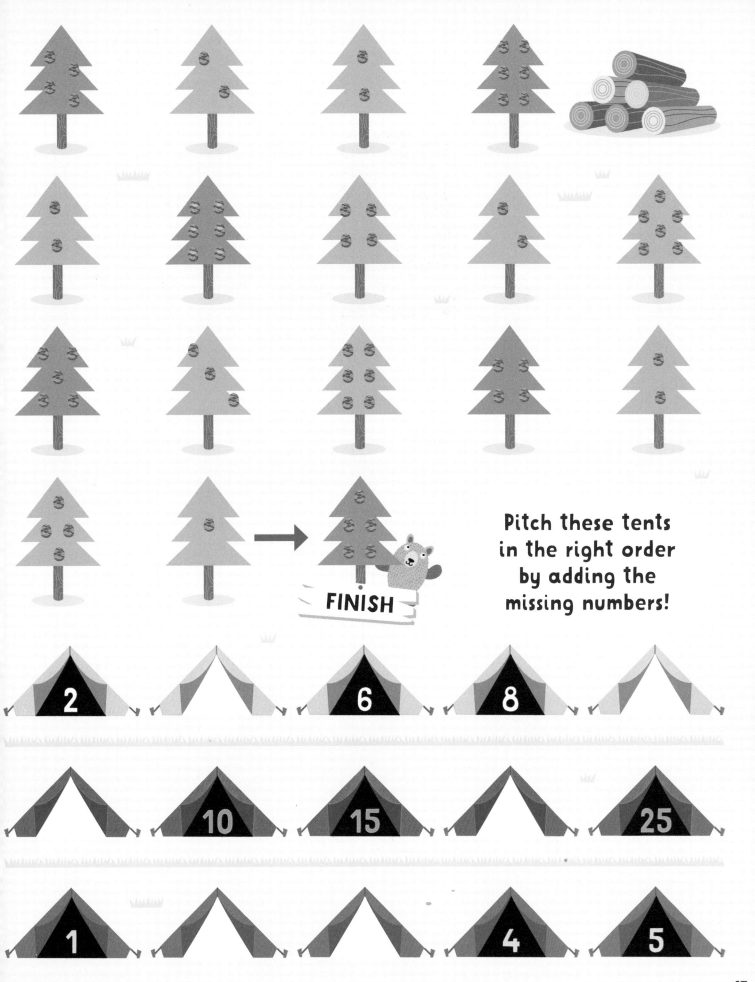

FINISH

Pitch these tents in the right order by adding the missing numbers!

| 2 | | 6 | 8 | |

| | 10 | 15 | | 25 |

| 1 | | | 4 | 5 |

I didn't catch any fish!
How many did you catch?

Can you help us finish serving the food?

Each plate should add up to **8**.

Draw the missing food items on the plates.

Fill in each blank by adding up
the two numbers above it—then run!

I'd better get out of here!

Who's trying to
escape the eruption?

Draw lines to match each dino with its nest.

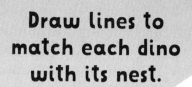

Hmm ... which nest is mine? I laid **10** eggs.

I laid **2** eggs fewer than Green Grace.

I laid **3** eggs more than Purple Penelope.

I laid half as many eggs as Red Rachel.

Help us build the pyramids by filling in the missing numbers.

Fill in each blank by adding up the numbers in the triangles on either side.

4 → 7 ← 3

10 items from the pharaoh's tomb!

What's missing?

Follow these directions to rescue the Duke!

X X 2 2 3 1

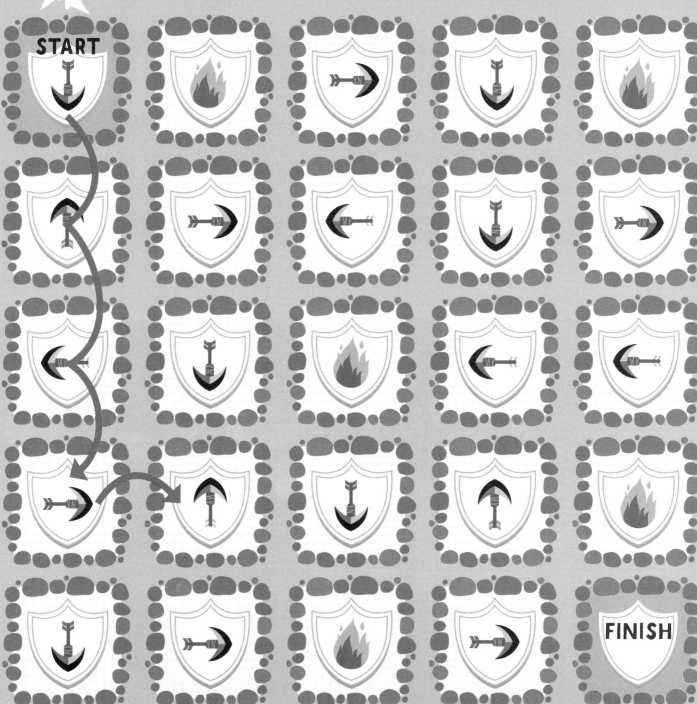

Caw! Use the color key
to finish the dragon.

29

We can still make it to the jousting tournament, Duke.

We'll need to collect **8** more coins on the way!

START

FINISH

Entry:
10 coins

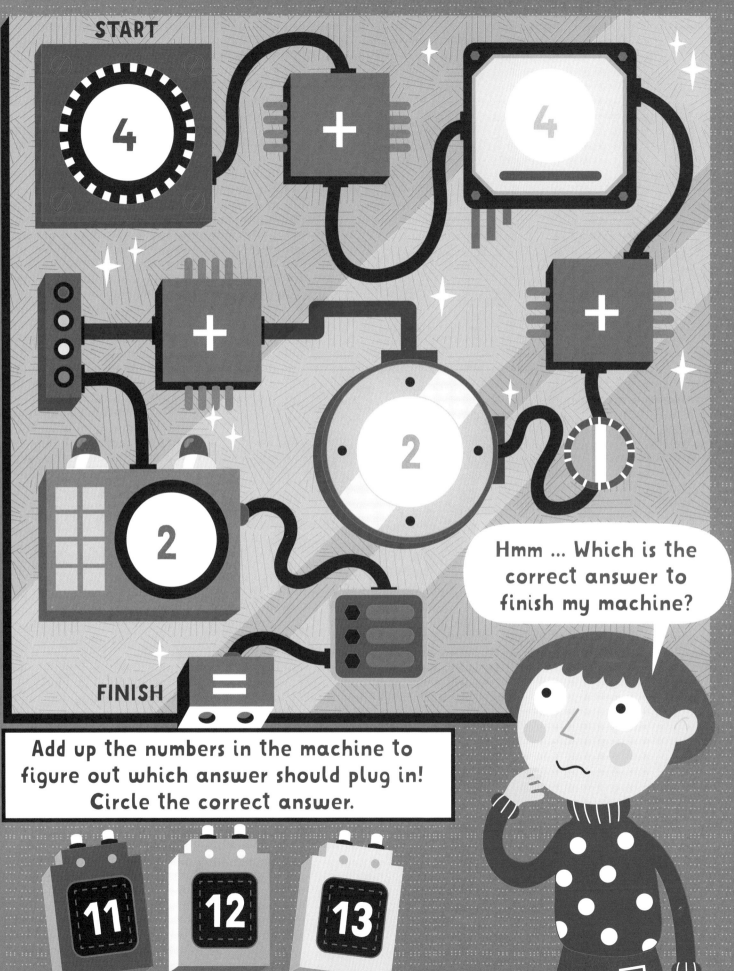

START

FINISH

Hmm ... Which is the correct answer to finish my machine?

Add up the numbers in the machine to figure out which answer should plug in! Circle the correct answer.

11   12   13

35

How many fans does each monster have?

My fans have brought banners! I've got _____ fans.

My fans are waving flags! I've got _____ fans.

My fans are wearing hats! I've got _____ fans.

Car color	Lap time (seconds)			
	1	+ 2	+ 3	= Total
Yellow	5	+ 10	+ 10	=
Orange	10	+ 5	+ 5	=
Green	10	+ 10	+ 10	=

... And they've done it! Add up the lap times to find the fastest and slowest times, then color the cars in the right colors.

I was the slowest ... but I had fun!

38

START

2

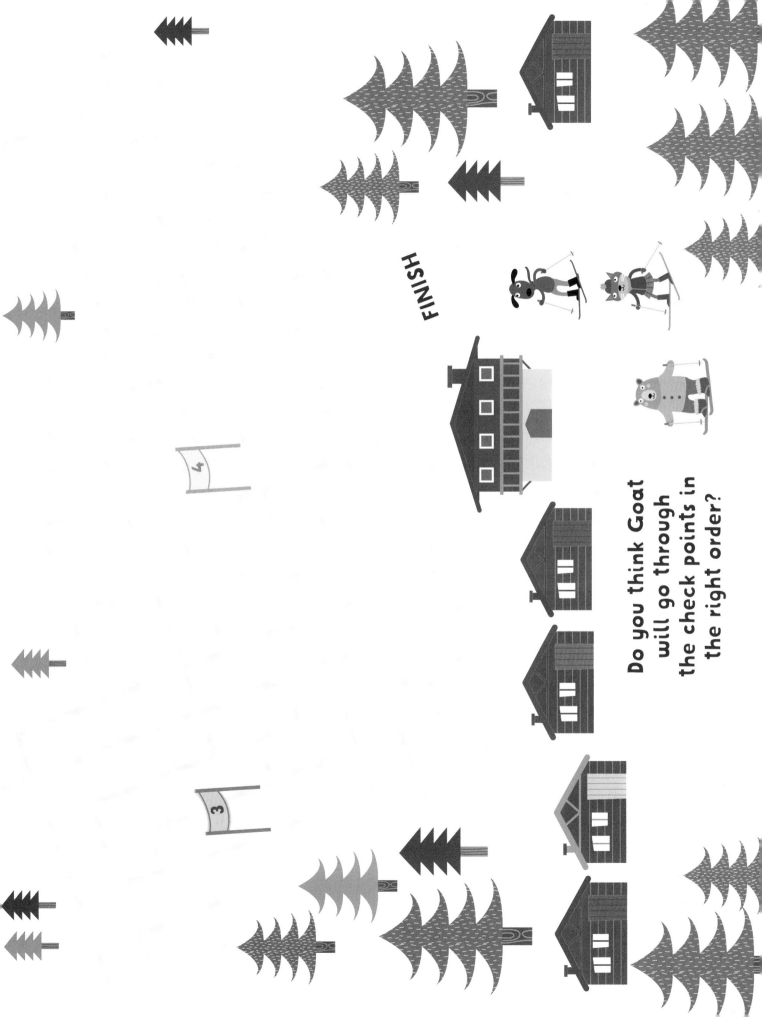

FINISH

Do you think Goat
will go through
the check points in
the right order?

Ride these cable cars
in the right order by adding
the missing numbers!

43

Draw lines to match each child with his or her bucket.

I have **2** shells in my bucket!

I have double the number of shells as Green Pippa.

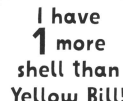

I have **1** more shell than Yellow Bill!

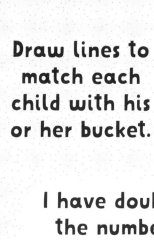

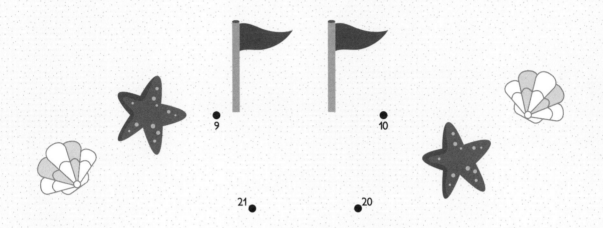

Look at what I've built!

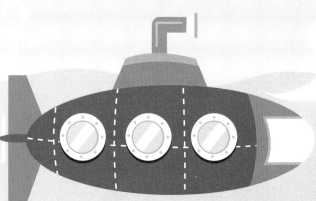

Follow these directions to find the rare puffer fish!

5 1 3 4

START

Use the color key to finish the picture.

1   2   3   4   5

10 sea creatures have left the reef for warmer waters!

50

Who's missing?

53

START

Go up, down, left, or right at the odd-numbered houses to get the delivery driver to the right house.

54

I'm getting really hungry!

FINISH

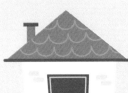

Plant the vegetables in the right order by adding the missing numbers to the signs.

Draw the missing veggies in the spaces!

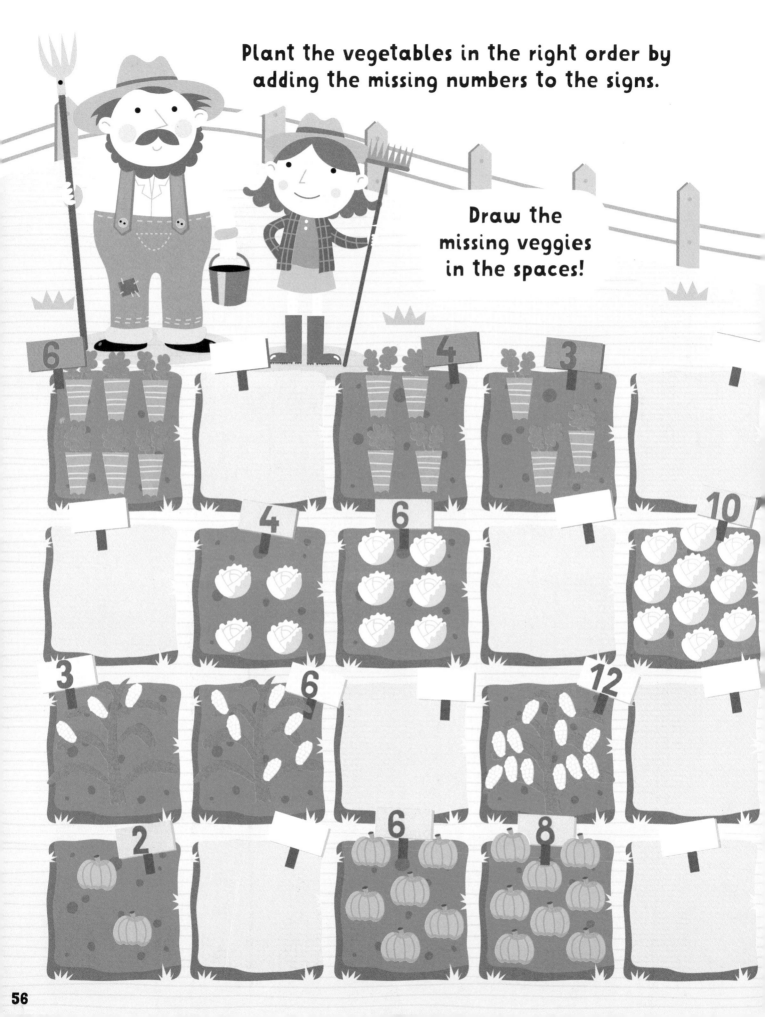

Caw! Fill in each blank by adding up the two numbers below it.

Bug spotter's guide:

2 black spiders ☐

1 red butterfly ☐

5 yellow dragonflies ☐

3 blue bugs ☐

8 green grasshoppers ☐

I only like flowers with **3** leaves!
Which one should I pick?

A

B

C

D

SUMMER

It's amazing! **10** of these birds will migrate for the winter!

WINTER

Brrr! Which birds have flown away?

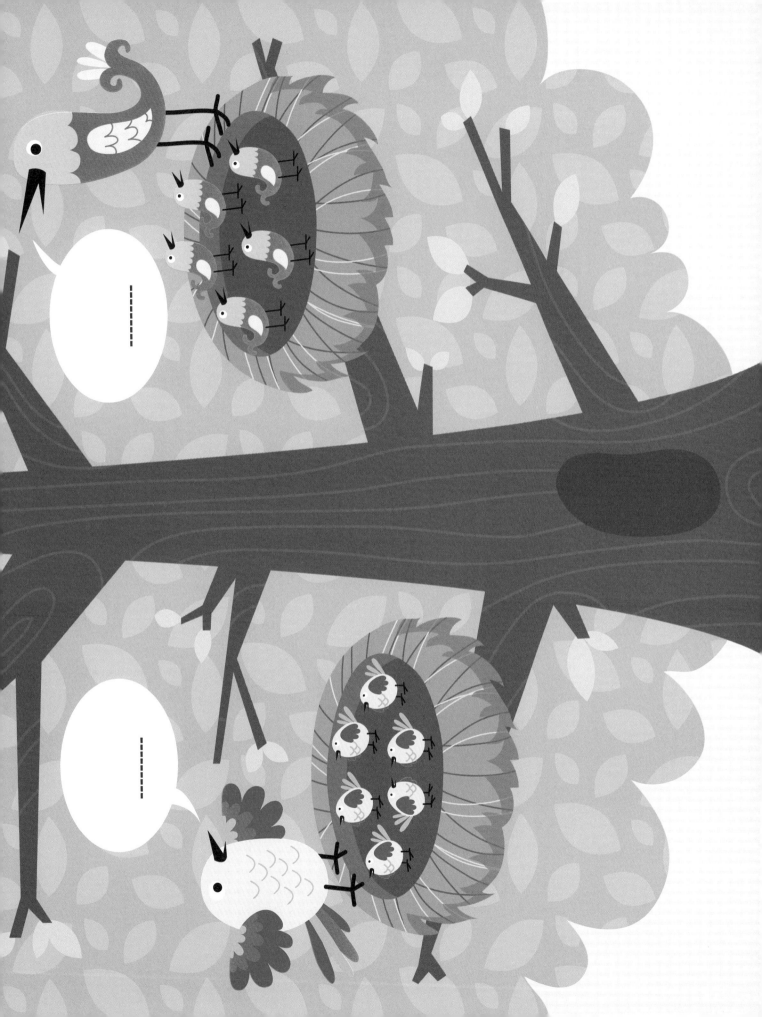

Who will meet the most giraffes on this safari? Follow each truck's matching arrows to find out!

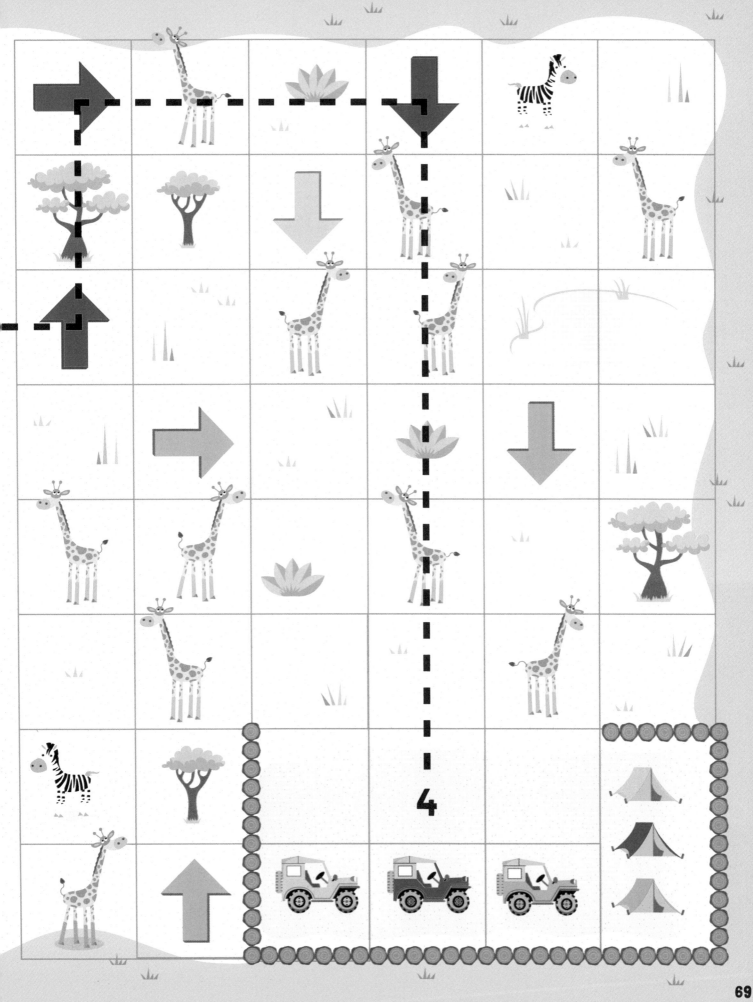

The monkeys took my glasses, too! What's peeping out of the leaves?

Use the color key to finish the picture.

1 2 3 4 5

It's nice to meet you! What are your names?

You can guess! We'll each give a clue to someone else's name.

Coral is holding **1** pink comb and has **2** orange starfish in her hair.

My name is

_____

Star has **3** stars on his top and **6** red scales on his tail.

My name is

_____

Pebble has **7** spots on his top and **1** strand of seaweed in his hair.

Madison has **2** shells in her hair.

My name is

My name is

Shelley has **4** green shells in her hair and a necklace with **5** purple jewels.

My name is

Who's the winner? Who has the highest total?

I've got **13**

I've got _____

5 3 4 2

I've got _____

7 3 1 2

I've got _____

6 1 4 2

Use the color key to finish the picture.

75

14-5-24-20   20-1-18-7-5-20

N _____   _____

9-19   20-8-5   2-1-14-11

_____   _____   _____

Quick! We need to
decode this secret
message to find the
robber's next target!

I have the code
breaker here!

A = 1	B = 2		D = 4
E = 5	F = 6	C = 3	H = 8
I = 9	J = 10	G = 7	L = 12
M = 13	N = 14	K = 11	P = 16
Q = 17	R = 18	O = 15	T = 20
U = 21	V = 22	S = 19	X = 24
Y = 25	Z = 26	W = 23	

Add up the minutes it takes to drive down each road to find the quickest route to the bank!

Red route: _____ Blue route: _____

POLICE LINEUP

1   **2**   **3**

Read the witness accounts to find the robber.

The robber had **1** pom-pom on his hat!

There were **7** spots on his pants!

The robber had **3** buttons on his coat!

4

5

6

There were **4** spots on each elbow pad.

He had **5** orange stripes on his t-shirt!

It was number _____ !

79

Draw lines to join up the coordinates to reveal the sacred temple!

B4   D4   D3   G6   D9   D8   B8   B4

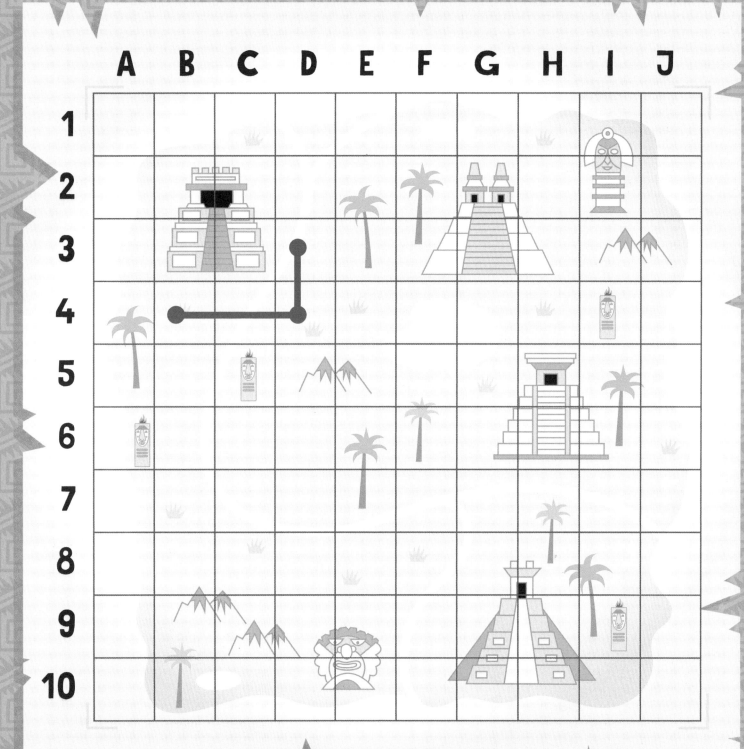

Use the code below to
find the answers and
unlock the temple door!

$8 + 7 - 6 =$

8   9

FINISH

Phew! The house is almost finished.
It should look exactly like these plans.

There are **8** jobs still to do. Circle them to help the builder finish the house!

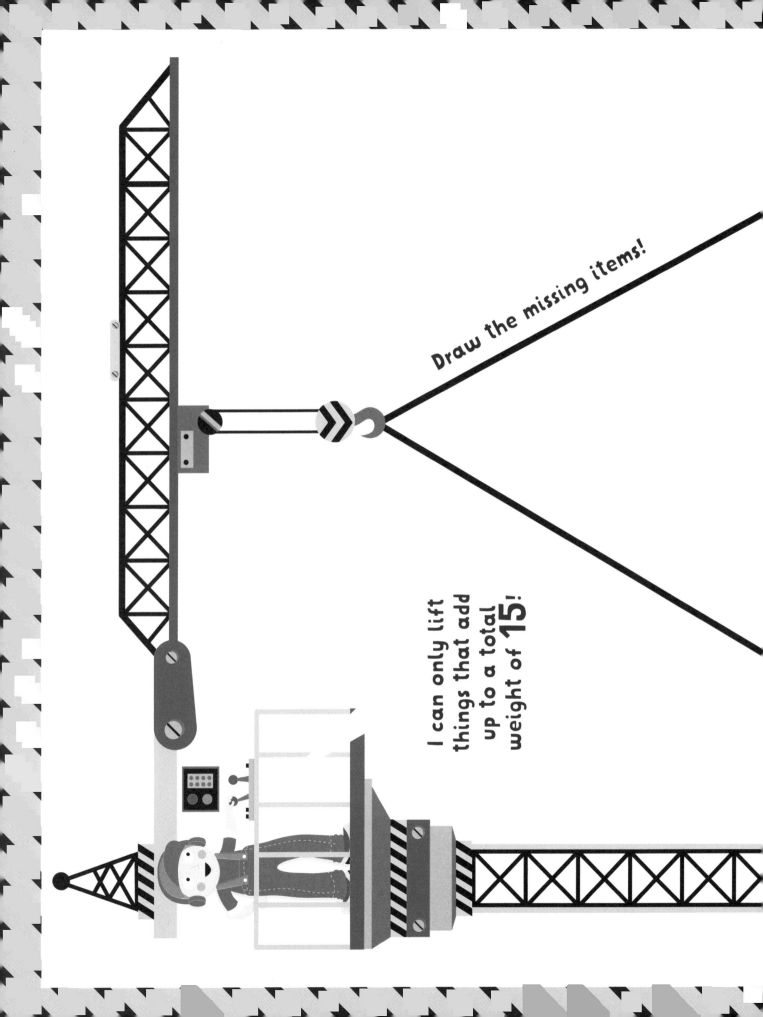

Draw the missing items!

I can only lift things that add up to a total weight of **15**!

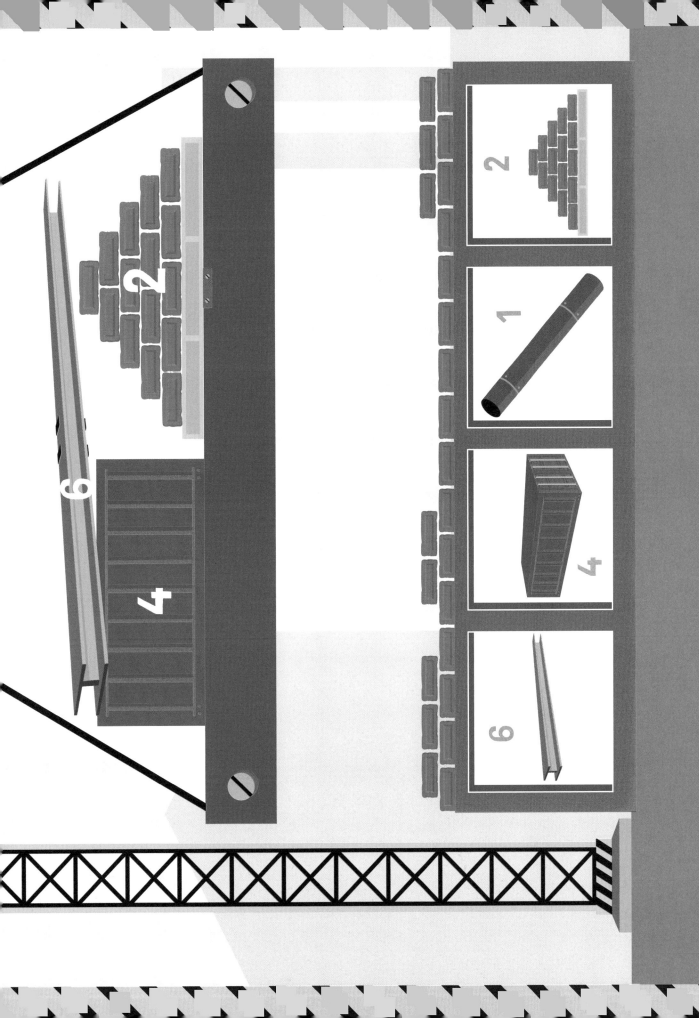

Draw lines to match each animal with his or her drum.

My drum has **7** stars.

My drum has **2** more stars than Elephant.

88

I have the most stars.

My drum has **5** stars fewer than Giraffe.

START

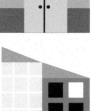

VEGETABLES

PARADE ROUTE:

Pass **4** houses, each with **2** windows.

Pass **2** shops selling vegetables.

Pass the fire station.

Pass **2** parked blue cars.

Pass **3** restaurants.

Pass **5** parked red cars.

Pass the café.

Where does the parade end?

BURGERS

DOUGHNUTS

PIZZA

FIRE STATION

VEGETABLES

SCHOOL

CAFÉ

TOWN HALL

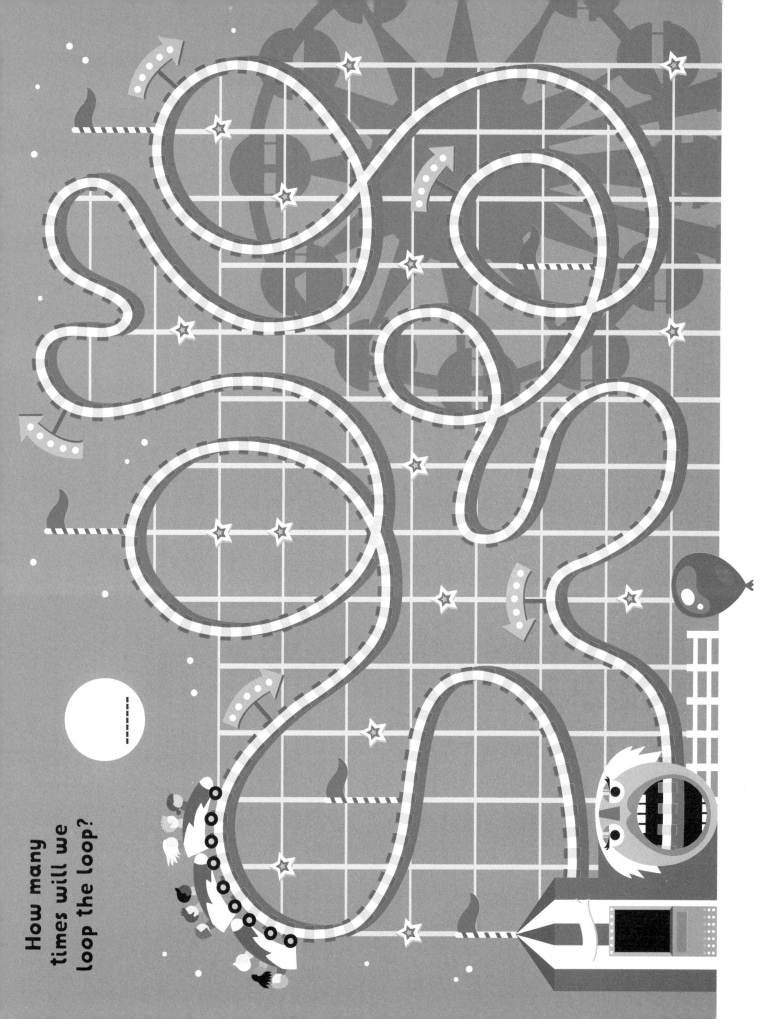

How many times will we loop the loop?

How many balloons has each stall sold today?

Who will win the trophy?

I won all the even-numbered prizes! How many did I get?

_____ even prizes

94

Draw lines to match each rancher to his or her herd of cattle.

I rounded up **2** more than Black-hat Bruce, but **1** fewer than Pink-hat Penny.

Whoa, boy! I rounded up **7** cows!

Come on, y'all—let's drive the cattle. We need to round up **6** cows!

START

FINISH

Draw a line to join each bolt to its wrench! The number of sides the bolt has matches the number on its wrench.

5

8

6

4

Fit the numbers below into the grid to help me find the new computer code (the numbers in the red squares).

38762   52729   3413526
17395   65284   2954984

Follow these coordinates to land the spacecraft.

C2 - B2 - B5 - D5 - D6 - E6 - E8

FINISH

105

Add up the score cards to find the highest and lowest scores, then write in the names of each pair.

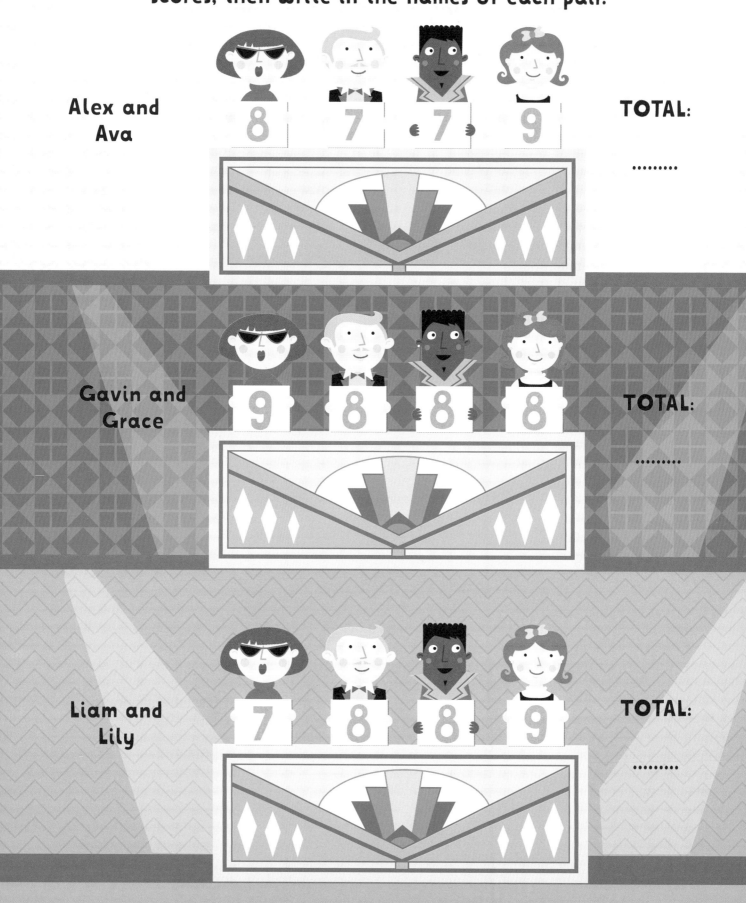

Alex and Ava — 8 7 7 9 — TOTAL: ....

Gavin and Grace — 9 8 8 8 — TOTAL: ....

Liam and Lily — 7 8 8 9 — TOTAL: ....

FINISH

FINISH

20 + 42 = ?

Pick the right key to escape
the haunted house.

53

72

62

73

52

61

63

71

I'd better lay these stones in the correct holes, or I'll be in big trouble with the Emperor!

I = 1
II = 2
III = 3
IV = 4
V = 5

II

IV

III

V

I

Solve the sums in the holes to find the correct stones.

I + II =

_____

V - IV =

_____

V - I =

_____

III + II =

_____

III - I =

_____

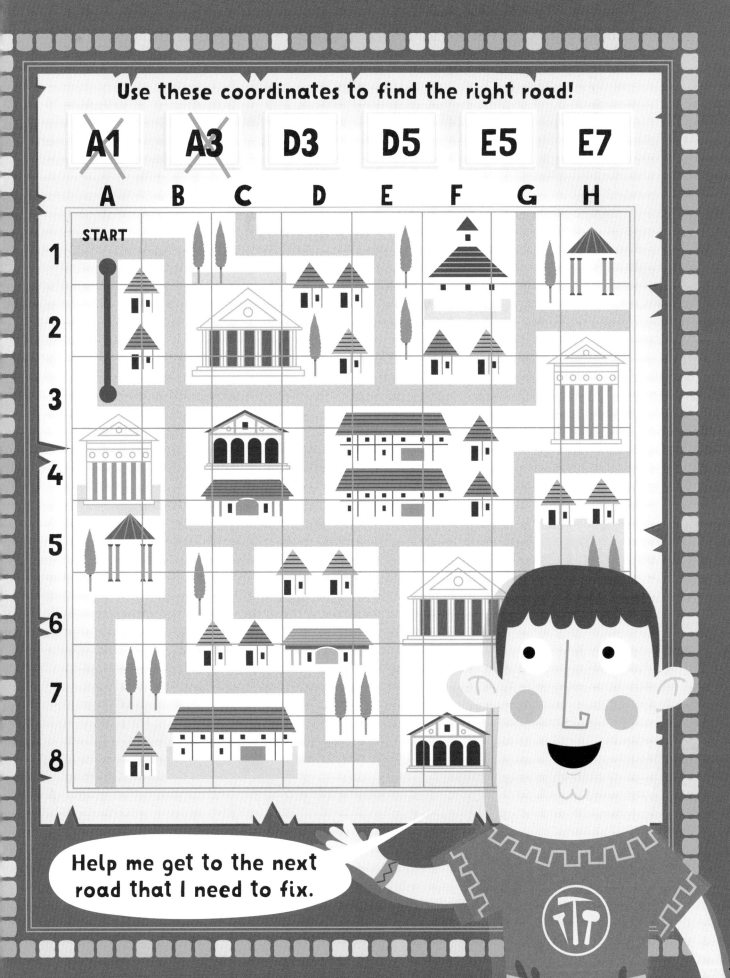

Help each passenger find his or her platform!

DEPARTURES		PLATFORM
10:45	Greenville	4
10:50	Springfield	5
10:55	Madison	7
11:00	Franklin	2
11:10	Washington	1
11:15	Salem	8
CURRENT TIME:		10:40

My train leaves in **5** minutes! I need to go to platform

....

I'm **30** minutes early for my train. I need to go to platform

....

My train leaves in **15** minutes. I need to go to platform

....

I'm **20** minutes early for my train. I need to go to platform

....

I can see **13**

_____

I can see **11**

_____

Play this game with a friend!

You will need:

2 counters + 1 die

How to play:

1. Each player puts their counter on the START square.

2. Take turns rolling the die. Move your counter forward the number of spaces shown on the die.

3. If your counter lands at the bottom of a hurdle, you can move up to the top of the hurdle.

4. The first player to get to the FINISH square is the winner.

FINISH
48 | 47 | 46

33 | 34 | 35

32 | 31 | 30

17 | 18 | 19

16 | 15 | 14

START
1 | 2 | 3

45	44	43	42	41
36	37	38	39	40
29	28	27	26	25
20	21	22	23	24
13	12	11	10	9
4	5	6	7	8

ANSWERS

Pages 4-5

Pages 6-7

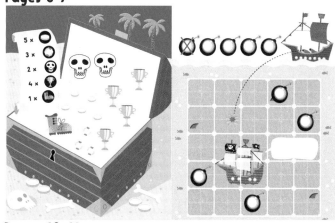

Pages 8-9

Pages 10-11

Pages 12-13

Pages 14-15

Pages 16-17

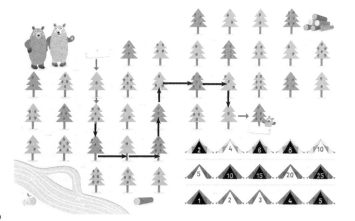

Pages 18-19

Pages 20-21

Pages 22-23

Pages 24-25

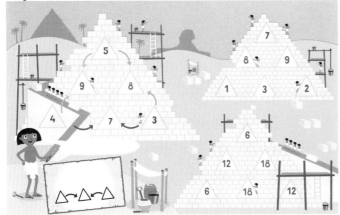

Pages 26-27

Pages 28-29

Pages 30-31

Pages 32-33

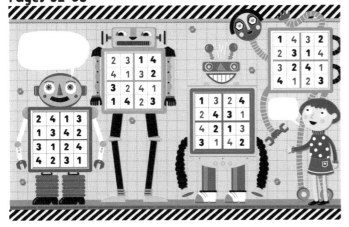

Pages 34-35

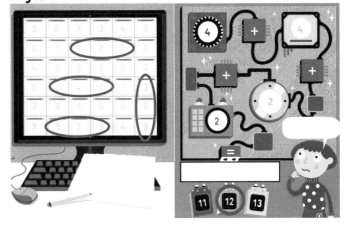

Pages 36-37

Pages 38-39

Pages 40-41

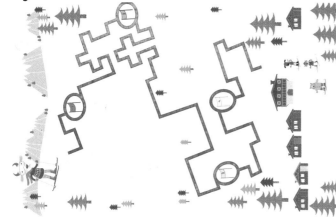

Pages 42-43

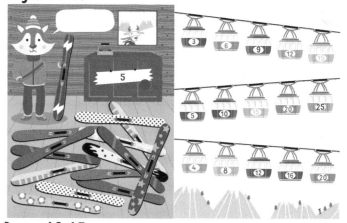

Pages 44-45

Pages 46-47

Pages 48-49

Pages 50-51

Pages 52-53

Pages 54-55

Pages 56-57

Pages 58-59

Pages 60-61

Pages 62-63

Pages 64-65

Pages 66-67

125

Pages 68-69

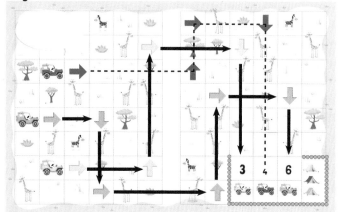

Pages 70-71

Pages 72-73

Pages 74-75

Pages 76-77

Pages 78-79

Pages 80-81

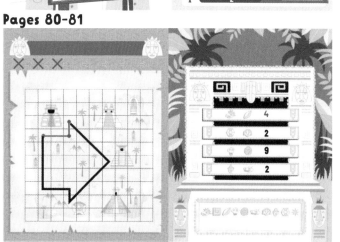

Pages 82-83

Pages 84-85

Pages 86-87

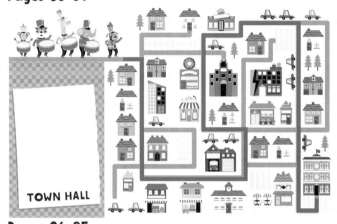

Pages 88-89

Pages 90-91

Pages 92-93

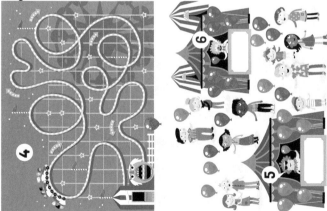

Pages 94-95

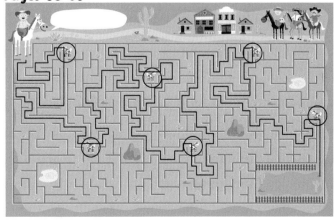

Pages 96-97

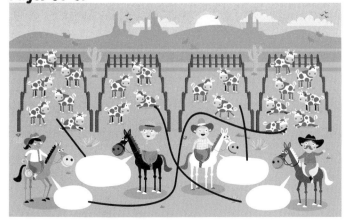

Pages 98-99

Pages 100-101

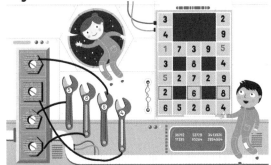

Pages 102-103

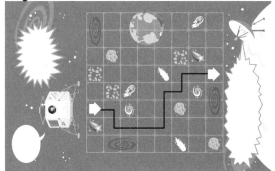

Pages 104-105

Pages 106-107

Pages 108-109

Pages 110-111

Pages 112-113

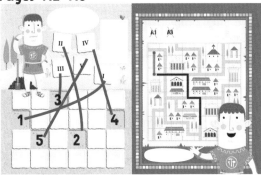

Pages 114-115

Pages 116-117

Pages 118-119